Popular Rock Superstars of Yesterday and Today
POP ROCK

AC/DC

Aerosmith

The Allman
Brothers Band

The Beatles

Billy Joel

Bob Marley
and the Wailers

Bruce Springsteen

The Doors

Elton John

The Grateful Dead

Led Zeppelin

Lynyrd Skynyrd

Pink Floyd

Queen

The Rolling
Stones

U2

The Who

The Grateful Dead

Kenneth McIntosh

Mason Crest Publishers

The Grateful Dead

FRONTIS From San Francisco came one of the most beloved bands in rock
  music—The Grateful Dead.

Produced by 21st Century Publishing and Communications, Inc.

Editorial by Harding House Publishing Services, Inc.

MASON CREST PUBLISHERS INC.
370 Reed Road
Broomall, Pennsylvania 19008
(866) MCP-BOOK (toll free)
www.masoncrest.com

Printed in the United States.

First Printing

9 8 7 6 5 4 3 2 1

Library of Congress Cataloging-in-Publication Data

McIntosh, Kenneth, 1959–
    The Grateful Dead / Kenneth McIntosh.
      p. cm. — (Popular rock superstars of yesterday and today)
    Includes bibliographical references (p.   ) and index.
    Hardback edition: ISBN-13: 978-1-4222-0191-6
    Paperback edition: ISBN-13: 978-1-4222-0314-9
  1. Grateful Dead (Musical group)—Juvenile literature. 2. Rock musicians—
United States—Biography—Juvenile literature. I. Title.
ML3930.G735M35 2008
782.42166092'2—dc22
[B]   2007012140

Publisher's notes:
  • All quotations in this book come from original sources, and contain the spelling
    and grammatical inconsistencies of the original text.

  • The Web sites mentioned in this book were active at the time of publication.
    The publisher is not responsible for Web sites that have changed their addresses
    or discontinued operation since the date of publication. The publisher will review
    and update the Web site addresses each time the book is reprinted.

CONTENTS

ROCK 'N' ROLL TIMELINE

1951
"Rocket 88," considered by many to be the first rock single, is released by Ike Turner.

1952
DJ Alan Freed coins and popularizes the term "Rock and Roll," proclaimes himself the "Father of Rock and Roll," and declares, "Rock and Roll is a river of music that has absorbed many streams: rhythm and blues, jazz, rag time, cowboy songs, country songs, folk songs. All have contributed to the Big Beat."

1955
"Rock Around the Clock" by Bill Haley & His Comets is released; it tops the U.S. charts and becomes wildly popular in Britain, Australia, and Germany.

1969
The Woodstock Music and Arts Festival attracts a huge crowd to rural upstate New York.

1969
Tommy, the first rock opera, is released by British rock band The Who.

1967
The Monterey Pop Festival in California kicks off open air rock concerts.

1965
The psychedelic rock band, the Grateful Dead, is formed in San Francisco.

1970
The Beatles break up.

1971
Jim Morrison, lead singer of The Doors, dies in Paris.

1971
Duane Allman, lead guitarist of the Allman Brothers Band, dies.

1950s   1960s   1970s

1957
Bill Haley tours Europe.

1957
Jerry Lee Lewis and Buddy Holly become the first rock musicians to tour Australia.

1954
Elvis Presley releases the extremely popular single "That's All Right (Mama)."

1961
The first Grammy for Best Rock 'n' Roll Recording is awarded to Chubby Checker for *Let's Twist Again*.

1964
The Beatles make their first visit to America, setting off the British Invasion.

1969
A rock concert held at Altamont Speedway in California is marred by violence.

1969
The Rolling Stones tour America as "The Greatest Rock and Roll Band in the World."

1973
Rolling Stone magazine names Annie Leibovitz chief photographer and "rock 'n' roll photographer;" she follows and photographs rockers Mick Jagger, John Lennon, and others.

1974
Sheer Heart Attack by the British rock band Queen becomes an international success.

1974
"Sweet Home Alabama" by Southern rock band Lynyrd Skynyrd is released and becomes an American anthem.

1987
Billy Joel becomes the first American rock star to perform in the Soviet Union since the construction of the Berlin Wall.

2005
Led Zeppelin is ranked #1 on VH1's list of the 100 Greatest Artists of Hard Rock.

2005
Many rock groups participate in Live 8, a series of concerts to raise awareness of extreme poverty in Africa.

1985
Rock stars perform at Live Aid, a benefit concert to raise money to fight Ethiopian famine.

2003
Led Zeppelin's "Stairway to Heaven" is inducted into the Grammy Hall of Fame.

1980
John Lennon of the Beatles is murdered in New York City.

2000s
Aerosmith's album sales reach 140 million worldwide and the group becomes the bestselling American hard rock band of all time.

2007
Billy Joel become the first person to sing the National Anthem before two Super Bowls.

1975
Tommy, the movie, is released.

1975
Time magazine features Bruce Springsteen on its cover as "Rock's New Sensation."

1995
The Rock and Roll Hall of Fame and Museum opens in Cleveland, Ohio.

1970s   1980s   1990s   2000s

1979
Pink Floyd's *The Wall* is released.

1991
Freddie Mercury, lead vocalist of the British rock group Queen, dies of AIDS.

2004
Elton John receives a Kennedy Center Honor.

1979
The first Grammy for Best Rock Vocal Performance by a Duo or Group is awarded to The Eagles.

2004
Rolling Stone Magazine ranks The Beatles #1 of the 100 Greatest Artists of All Time, and Bob Dylan #2.

1986
The Rolling Stones receive a Grammy Lifetime Achievement Award.

1981
MTV goes on the air.

2006
U2 wins five more Grammys, for a total of 22—the most of any rock artist or group.

1981
For Those About to Rock We Salute You by Australian rock band AC/DC becomes the first hard rock album to reach #1 in the U.S.

1986
The first Rock and Roll Hall of Fame induction ceremony is held; Chuck Berry, Little Richard, Ray Charles, Elvis Presley, and James Brown, are among the first inductees.

2006
Bob Dylan, at age 65, releases *Modern Times* which immediately rises to #1 in the U.S.

The
GRATEFUL DEAD
★ **PERFORMING LIVE** ★

SAN FRANCISCO

12:00 NOON - 3:00 P. M.

★ ★ ★ **SPECIAL GUEST** ★ ★ ★

During the 1960s, a flyer for a Grateful Dead concert would also tell concertgoers that a good time would be had by all. Good music would be plentiful, and so would drugs (especially LSD) and alcohol, two major players in the acid rock–hippy world of that era. The Grateful Dead seemed tailor-made for the scene.

1

Long, Strange Trip

Like children pursuing the Pied Piper, they come. Some stand long hours on dusty byways, thumbs out, hoping and praying someone will give them a lift. Others drive Volkswagen vans; tires worn, motors smoking, plastered with stickers—pictures of dancing bears, skulls and roses, and slogans like *Forever Grateful* and *Keep on Truckin'*.

Groups of young people ride together in brightly painted busses, eating and sleeping on the road, in cramped interiors smelling of Patchouli and incense. From around the world, they follow the music.

Deadheads

They pull into an enormous field, parking space for the show. There, they disentangle their cramped bodies from vehicles and begin the gathering rituals.

The parking lot turns into a small, festive village. Merchants set up tents covering tables full of cassette recordings, tie-dyed T-shirts, jewelry, and drug paraphernalia. Travelers gather in clusters, share stories, eat, drink, smoke, play hand-drums, and dance.

It is a portable community of college students and dropouts, freaks and working people, groupies, artists, musicians, and regular Joes and Janes. Some come from nearby, leaving their everyday world only for a short time, yet others are truly Dead-icated, shaping their lives so they can follow the band from show to show. They are a diverse tribe, yet a common love unites them. They are devotees of what Robert Hunter (Grateful Dead songwriter) calls, "A religion without beliefs."

A Rainbow Full of Sound

Dusk settles; the crowd streams into the show. Some stand outside, with signs—*I need a miracle!* These unfortunates have no tickets; they wish for someone to sell them extras (hopefully not at a jacked-up price). If they cannot buy their way in, they may try other ways to enter the show after dark: climb the high fence or find a broken place to crawl through . . . whatever they have to do to reach the Promised Land beyond the gates.

Inside, fans wait eagerly. And then . . . light shines from the darkness onto the stage. Whistles from the audience mingle with seemingly random musical notes: the sound of drums, guitars, and a keyboard searching for a common musical direction. Center stage, a spotlight focuses on Jerry Garcia, the heart of the Dead. He glances shyly at the crowd, his round spectacles, unruly mass of white hair, and Santa Claus beard gleaming in the lights.

Jerry caresses the neck of his guitar, handmade by Doug Irwin. This beautiful instrument is Jerry's magic wand, his closest companion; he practically sleeps with it. The road crew might break or lose band property—that's okay—but never, heaven help them, Jerry's guitar.

Beside him is Bob Weir, clean-shaven, ruggedly handsome; while Jerry noodles, Bob strums chords on his Telecaster®. On Jerry's other side, Phil Lesh, thin and **bespectacled**, plays bass guitar. Behind them, Bill Kreutzmann and Mickey Hart pound out rhythm.

Settling into a tune, the Grateful Dead begins to weave a musical, mystical spell that captivates the audience. For hours, those in the crowd dance and sway, entranced. Musicians and audience play off each other's moods. More than any other band, the Dead and its followers together create the vibe of a show.

The night moves along like a musical journey, always changing. The Dead is famous for the way its members **improvise**; no two shows

Grateful Dead audiences were huge—and enthusiastic. Dedicated Deadheads would travel hundreds of miles— sometimes more—to experience a Grateful Dead concert. At times, it appeared as though Deadheads were packed shoulder-to-shoulder into the concert venue. But the crowd didn't mind; they were all there to share their love with the Dead.

Each Grateful Dead concert was a unique experience because the group seldom played its songs the same way twice. Jerry and the others took their cues from the audience; as the crowd went, so did the band. Few rock groups of that time or since have depended so much on the crowd to inspire its performance.

are ever the same. They play old folk tunes like "Peggy-O," and spaced-out electronic innovations such as "Terrapin Station." Some songs are somber tearjerkers like "Broke Down Palace," with its soulful "fare thee well" chorus. Others are on-your-feet rockers like "Sugar Magnolia." Bill and Mickey create a hypnotic pulse jamming on an array of percussion instruments. Caught up in this extravaganza of sounds, folks in the audience forget themselves and become part of a greater whole for the evening.

So Many Roads

Over the course of thirty years, from 1965 to 1995, the Grateful Dead became America's most successful touring act, even performing in front of Egypt's great pyramids. In 1994, the Dead was inducted into the Rock and Roll Hall of Fame; yet it never became a top-40 pop group. The band made a fortune touring, but it also spent vast amounts of money for a small army of roadies and technicians.

The Dead story is one of great comedy and tragedy. The band and fans had lofty goals—love, peace, and universal compassion. At the same time, awful things happened—relationships and marriages broken, fatalities related to drugs and alcohol, and several lawsuits filed after Jerry's death. Like life itself, the Grateful Dead saga is full of contradictions.

Ultimately, it's about the music. Jerry said,

"We need magic, and bliss, and power, myth, and celebration and religion in our lives, and music is a good way to encapsulate a lot of it."

Blair Jackson, publisher of *The Golden Road* magazine, wrote of Jerry,

"There was nothing he liked more than playing music in a band in front of dancing people. He didn't care if the group was acoustic or electric or if the audience was large or small—it was all about hearts and souls coming together through music."

The band, their devotees, and their music told a single saga—the Grateful Dead story.

BOOK OF THE DEAD

Celebrating 25 Years with the Grateful Dead

The 1960s was a decade of unrest, and a generation of young people went in search of ways to make the world better. Some believed music and wild dancing could make the world a better place. Drugs and psychedelic lights were sometimes used to enhance the experience. And the Grateful Dead participated in it all!

2

The Dead Come Alive

They called themselves the "Beat" generation—as in "upbeat" and "**beatific**." This group of writers, students, and travelers burst the limits of personal and artistic freedom in the 1950s. At the time, many older people looked down on writer Jack Kerouac, poet Alan Ginsberg, and outrageous character Neal Cassady, because in square America, these beatniks broke every rule.

Catching the Beat

They lived to travel, because, to quote Kerouac, "The road is life." They were into drugs, sex, and jazz (as in, "Be-bopp baby, blow cat, blow!"). As Kerouac said,

> **"the only people for me are the mad ones, the ones who are mad to live, mad to talk . . . who . . . burn, burn, burn, like fabulous yellow roman candles exploding."**

The Beats led lives full of drama. They rebelled against society and created a new way of living—in some ways better, in other ways worse than the lifestyle they rejected. Exploring the limits of alcohol and drugs, they saw the best and brightest among them struggle with addiction and death. Pursuing freedom was their highest value, and many Beats left a trail of abandoned spouses and neglected children in their wake. The hippies, who were the second generation of beatniks, carried on with the same kinds of blessings and curses.

Many of today's teens are unaware of the Beat generation, despite the fact that Beat influenced the Doors, R.E.M., U2, Nirvana, the Beastie Boys—and the Grateful Dead. You can blame the Beats for ruining lives or praise them for reinventing culture; either way, they changed our world.

Jerry's Role Model

As a teen, Jerry read Kerouac's *On the Road*. He said that book was "the turning point of my life." *On the Road* gave Jerry a hero, Dean Moriarity, modeled on real-life adventurer Neal Cassady.

Cassady **enthralled** his peers. He was not a great artist, musician, or writer. In fact, his only real skills seemed to be driving cars and talking nonstop. Yet he drew people to him—inspiring writers, musicians, and philosophers. Women found him irresistible. Neal was determined to experience everything life offered, no matter how dangerous. For better or worse, Jerry chose Neal Cassady for his role model. Garcia soon had the opportunity to meet his hero, as they both lived in San Francisco. However, Cassady died a few years later, at the age of forty-one, lying alone on train tracks in a cold rain, drunk after a party in Mexico.

A Band Beyond Description

You can think of members of the Grateful Dead as the cast of a long-running television series, one that stayed on the air for thirty years. The show began with five main characters (Jerry, Pigpen,

Bob, Phil, and Bill). Mickey joined the show in the third season, and Pigpen died in season six. Jerry, Bob, Phil, Bill, and Mickey played together from 1967 to 1995, while a half-dozen other members came and went.

The five original members of the Dead gathered in 1965. Though their personalities and styles varied greatly, they were all serious musicians. Jerry started playing guitar in 1957, when he talked his

The original Grateful Dead (shown here on a San Francisco street) met up in 1965. But, like many groups of the time, members came and went as if going through a revolving door—sometimes by mutual agreement, sometimes not. Though personalities differed, band members shared at least one thing in common—they loved music.

parents into getting him a six-string rather than their preference—an accordion. Jerry recalled,

> **"I went nuts—'Ahhhggg! No! No!'—I railed and I raved, and [my mother] finally turned it in, and I got a pawnshop electric guitar and an amplifier. I was beside myself with joy. . . . I wanted to make that sound so badly."**

Beginning in 1962, Jerry played folk music with Ron McKernan, better known as Pigpen. Pigpen sported a black beard, long hair, and

With his long hair and beard, Ron McKernan—Pigpen— certainly looked the part of a counterculture rock star. He also had talent. Bob Weir met Jerry when he followed the sound of a banjo into a music store and found the future band leader. They knew they were going to start a band after that first jam session.

wore a curled-up cowboy hat and boots. A well-rounded musician, he belted out powerful vocals, played guitar, keyboard, and harmonica.

Meanwhile, Bill Kreutzmann had been banging on drums since the age of eight, was kicked out of sixth-grade orchestra for not keeping time, and took lessons as a result. He stopped in at Dana Morgan's music store in 1962 to sell a banjo to a young man who taught there—Jerry Garcia. Three years later, when Jerry was forming a band, he asked Bill to play drums.

Bob Weir was not a great high school student (he is **dyslexic**), but he was an outstanding guitar player. On New Year's Eve 1963, sixteen-year-old Bob was strolling through Palo Alto, California, looking for a club that would admit an underaged kid, when he heard banjo music. He followed the sound to Dana Morgan's Music Store, where Jerry Garcia, amazingly unaware of the holiday, waited for students to arrive. Bob and Jerry spent the night playing music together, then decided to start a band. It was first called Mother McCree's Uptown Jug Champions, but they soon changed that name to the Warlocks.

In 1965, Phil Lesh was a formally trained jazz player (violin and trumpet) newly acquainted with the wonders of LSD. A friend invited him and his girlfriend to a show by the Warlocks at a Menlo Park pizza joint called Magoo's. As they entered, Phil later said, he found "The music was so loud . . . the groove so compelling, that I just *had* to dance." Afterward, Phil talked to Jerry, who invited him to join the band and play bass. Phil had never played bass before, but Jerry knew he would quickly get the hang of it.

The Other One

In December of 1965, Phil discovered another band was out there named the Warlocks, so they had to change names. Gathered together, they tried out different ideas. Jerry opened an encyclopedia, thumbed through, and said, "Hey man, how about the Grateful Dead?" (The phrase comes from a Mexican holiday called *Dia de los Muertos*, Day of the Dead, when food, flowers, and other gifts are left on graves for the "grateful dead.")

Phil jumped up and down with excitement. "That's it!"

A few years later, in 1967, Mickey Hart, formerly a drummer for the Air Force Band, was at a performance by jazz great Count Basie when someone said, "You should meet Bill Kreutzmann, drummer for the

Though Phil Lesh was trained in violin and trumpet, Jerry knew he would be a good—even great—bass player. And as usual when it came to this kind of thing, Jerry was right. Mickey Hart was already an established drummer when he joined the Grateful Dead, but with Jerry and the others, Mickey found greater fame.

Grateful Dead." Mickey and Bill hit it off right away. The rest of the evening, the two strolled through town, banging on light poles, fences, cars—sharing beats and rhythms. Soon after, Mickey joined the Dead. After their first gig together Jerry walked over, hugged Mickey, and said, "*This* is the Grateful Dead; we can take *this* all over the world!"

Trippin'
The Beats used drugs to explore the limits of human experience. Most of them were college-educated artists, and they thought of drugs as "research" for their poetry and fiction.

Author Ken Kesey served as a "living bridge" between the beatniks of the 1950s and hippies of the 1960s. Kesey was a writer studying at Stanford University in 1959 when he volunteered to take part in a government study at a local veterans hospital. The study required those involved to take LSD, a drug popularly known as "acid." This drug sends takers on "trips" that creates strange sights, such as moving patterns, brilliant colors, and trails behind moving objects.

Around the same time, Dr. Timothy Leary received grant money from Harvard University to experiment with LSD; he gave thousands of doses to hundreds of people. The government soon shut down LSD experiments, but Leary and Kesey continued to give out samples of the drug (it was not illegal until October 1966).

A group of friends called the Merry Pranksters gathered at Kesey's ranch in the early sixties. The Pranksters included the legendary Neal Cassady and Mountain Girl, the woman who later became one of Jerry Garcia's wives. In 1964, the Pranksters painted an old bus and named it *Further*. With Cassady at the wheel, driving like a madman and talking even faster, they set out across the country, handing out acid and "turning on" countless young people along their way.

Members of the Grateful Dead—except for Pigpen, who preferred liquor—were enthusiastic takers of the new drug. They thought it would free them from the physical realm and give them new creative ideas. Jerry was especially turned on by the drug, earning him the nickname "Captain Trips."

Can You Pass the Acid Test?

The Pranksters held "acid tests," where partygoers took LSD, at various places around the country. These events were advertised with crayoned signs asking, "Can you pass the acid test?" The first acid test took place in Palo Alto in November 1965.

The idea of the acid tests was to create an entirely new kind of experience—and this required new sights and sounds. Hundreds of young people on LSD crowded into a large room where strobe lights flashed and the members of what would be later known as the Grateful Dead played new forms of music, enhancing the LSD trips. Young people in bright clothes with wild hairstyles danced for hours, lost to the world around them. Phil and other members of the

Dead believed that this "combination of music and ecstatic dancing is somehow making the world *better*."

Nearly forty years later, Grateful Dead biographer Dennis McNally said in an interview with *Salon* that one of the few positive benefits of the Dead's LSD use was that it redirected

> **their notion of what they were up to, and it made them understand that the audience was not separate from them, but was part of their experience, that they were partners. And that, in fact, the Grateful Dead was not six guys on stage, but everybody in the room and the instruments and the sound system. . . . It's dangerous about LSD because everybody experiences it differently, but one of the common conclusions people come to is a sense of the one-ness of all life. . . . And what [the band] decided was that there was loop of energy—it starts from the string and goes through the sound system and out into the audience and comes back—which is why they were notoriously a wonderful band live, frequently magical live, but in the studio without that feedback they were so-so.**

For these drug-driven shows, members of the Dead combined their skills playing jazz, folk, and **blues**, creating a unique musical blend. This new psychedelic music—sometimes called "acid rock"—influenced other San Francisco bands, including Jefferson Airplane and Big Brother and the Holding Company (the legendary Janis Joplin's group).

In *The Electric Kool-Aid Acid Test*, author Tom Wolfe described the experience of combining an acid test with a light show and the Dead's music:

> **The . . . light machine pitching the intergalactic red science-fiction seas to all corners of the lodge, oil and water and food coloring pressed between plates of glass and projected in vast size so that the very ooze of cellular Creation seems to ectoplast into the ethers**

MERRY PRANKSTERS & THE GRATEFUL DEAD

Signs such as the one shown in this photo announced one of the infamous Merry Pranksters acid tests. Members of the Grateful Dead were often in attendance at these parties, where drugs and bright lights combined with music and dancing to create an all-new experience. Some believed the experience would expand their creativity.

Pulsating, large, colorful, psychedelic images; guitar sounds that seemed to come from out of this world; an unusual blending of jazz, blues, and folk music: was that the ingredients of a nightmare? No, it was acid rock as performed by the Grateful Dead during the 1960s.

and then the Dead coming in with their immense submarine vibrato. . . . The Dead's weird sound! . . . tremendously loud but like sitting under a waterfall, at the same time full of sort of ghoul-show vibrato sounds as if each string on their electric guitars is half a block long and twanging in a room full of natural gas, not to mention their great Hammond electric organ, which sounds like a movie house Wurlitzer, a diathermy machine, a Citizen's Band radio and an Auto-Grind garbage truck at 4 A.M., all coming over the same frequency. ❞

Forty years later, we look back at the acid tests and ask, "*What* were they thinking?" We have to remember they didn't yet understand the destructive power of these drugs. For the Grateful Dead and others at the time, acid and marijuana were fresh sources of inspiration. They could not foresee that in the coming decades, drug addictions would hinder their music and cause tragic deaths.

In the middle of the sixties, the first hippies were turning on to new ways of thinking, moving ahead the social experiments of the Beat generation before them. The Grateful Dead had just begun the long, strange musical trip that would take them through countless joys and trials in the years to come.

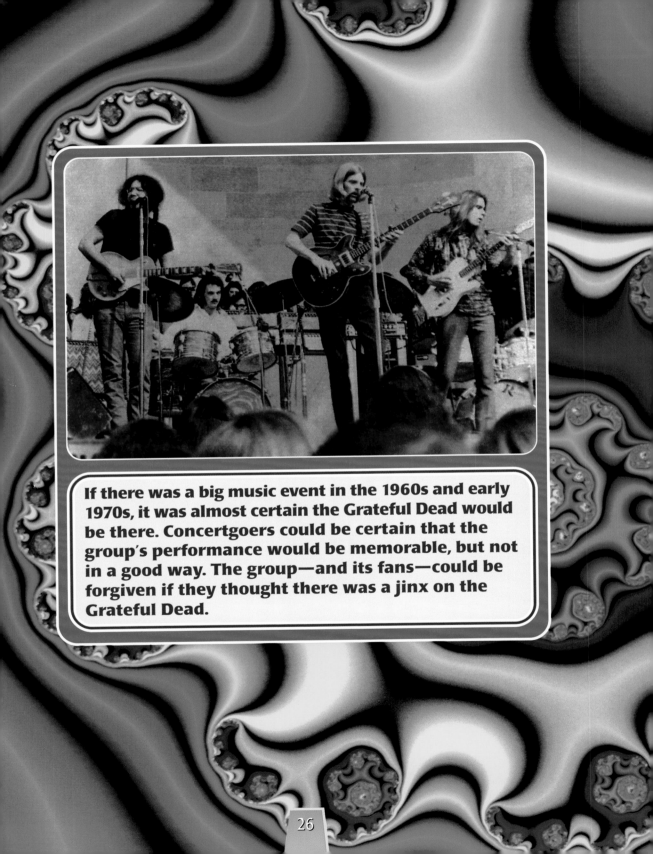

If there was a big music event in the 1960s and early 1970s, it was almost certain the Grateful Dead would be there. Concertgoers could be certain that the group's performance would be memorable, but not in a good way. The group—and its fans—could be forgiven if they thought there was a jinx on the Grateful Dead.

3

The Band Keeps Playin' On

In 1966, it seemed like the whole West Coast was magically changing. The acid tests were just one small part of an entire revolution in the way young people thought and lived. The hippie movement was beginning—and it was even bigger, bolder, and more colorful than their models, the Beats.

710 Ashbury

In the fall of '66, the Grateful Dead, along with friends, moved into 710 Ashbury Street in San Francisco. At the time, Haight-Ashbury was the hottest place in the revolution. Janis Joplin moved in for a brief but wholehearted romance with Pigpen. The Dead's pad was the happening place to be. As Phil recalls,

"I was in hog heaven; all I had to do was hang out . . . and play music. . . . There was truly magic in the air those days; everyone seemed to know and love one another."

When the Dead headlined for Bill Graham, a legendary promoter of rock acts at Fillmore West in '66, it had reached the big time. This was when the group also released its first single, "Don't Ease Me In." In March 1967, the band released its first album, *The Grateful Dead.*

Summer of Love

The biggest concert event of that year was June's Monterey Pop Festival. Almost 250,000 people enjoyed three days of music, including such acts as Jefferson Airplane, Janis Joplin, the Who, and Jimi Hendrix.

At Monterey, the Dead began its long tradition of "blowing the big ones." Whenever given a truly historic opportunity—huge crowds, a movie being recorded, a famous event—the band choked. At Monterey, the group played a poor set—and then Jimi Hendrix followed them onstage and gave a legendary performance.

The summer of '67 in San Francisco is called "the summer of love." Thousands of young people descended on the city to check out the scene. They came with little money and no place to stay, but with bags of grass in their bell-bottom jeans. They were looking for love and music. Sadly, other people were ready to take advantage of them. The summer of love resulted in a long list of rapes, rip-offs, and broken dreams. For those in the midst of the revolution, it was a warning: you can't just take crowds of people, mix with plenty of drugs, casual sex, and music—and achieve happiness. The problems of humanity weren't going to go away, not for the Grateful Dead, and not for their fans.

Darkness Falls at Altamont

The year 1969 saw the very best—and very worst—events of the decade: Woodstock and Altamont.

For three incredible days, half a million young people gathered at Max Yasgur's farm in Upstate New York to celebrate peace and love. The air was filled with nonstop legendary musical talent: Santana;

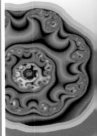

In August 1969, rock 'n' roll came to the countryside of Upstate New York—in a big way. More than 500,000 young people came to Woodstock to experience a three-day musical extravaganza. The biggest names in music were there, including the Who, Janis Joplin, Jimi Hendrix, and the Grateful Dead.

Janis Joplin; the Who; Jefferson Airplane; Crosby, Stills, Nash & Young; and Jimi Hendrix.

In addition to these other great acts, the Grateful Dead took the stage at Woodstock and—wouldn't you know it—played badly. The rain fried the band's electric connections; instruments and amplifiers cut out suddenly; and strange voices kept cutting in, making it impossible for the band to perform well. Woodstock was a shining moment in history—but not for the Dead.

In December of '69, promoters attempted another monster concert, this time at Altamont Raceway in Alameda County, California. If Woodstock was heaven, Altamont was descent into the inferno. The promoters hired the Hells Angels motorcycle club for security and paid for their services with beer—lots of it.

Fans shoved forward toward the stage. The Hells Angels had lined up their bikes to serve as a temporary fence, but people kept pushing into the bikes. There's nothing more precious to a Hells Angel than his chopper, so the Angels fought back savagely. The area in front of the show turned into a battle zone; throughout the day and into the night, Hells Angels and angry fans clashed violently.

When the Dead was supposed to go onstage, an angry Hells Angel stopped the group, so they decided not to play. Unfortunately, the Rolling Stones chose to continue the concert. The fighting grew worse. In the midst of the Stones' song "Under My Thumb," a couple of Hells Angels stabbed a man to death, just in front of the stage.

It was a sickening disappointment for the Dead. Everything the hippie movement stood for—love, peace—Altamont destroyed. The band responded to this horror by writing the song "New Speedway Boogie" about the concert at Altamont. In the song they regret that, "Things went down we don't understand," and end with the plea, "One way or another, this darkness got to give."

Drivin' That Train

In 1970, the Grateful Dead played 142 shows, the second-highest number in any year of its three decades on the road. The most famous performances were a series of concerts at Bill Graham's Fillmore East. One particularly memorable evening, members of the Allman Brothers Band and Fleetwood Mac joined the Dead onstage. But even more opportunities were coming their way.

Members of the Grateful Dead associated trains with the great American folk music tradition, so railroads were very cool. They were delighted, therefore, when asked to join the Transcontinental Pop Festival, also known as the Festival Express, traveling by rail across Canada. Along with Janis Joplin and other performers, they rode on a passenger train from performance to performance.

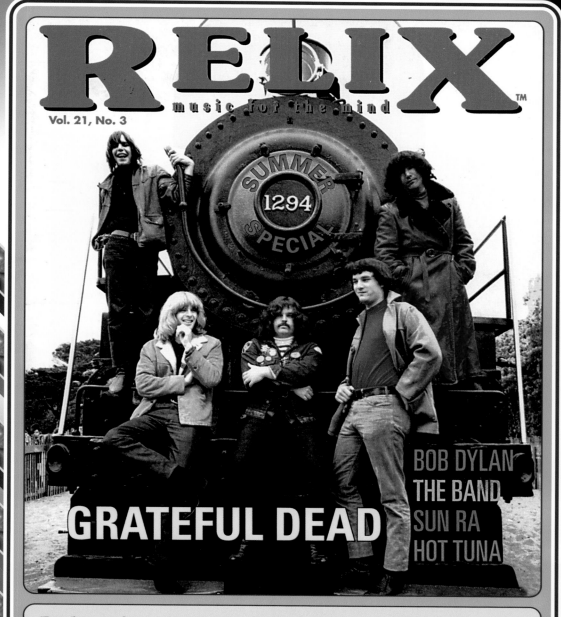

RELIX
music for the mind
Vol. 21, No. 3

SUMMER 1294 SPECIAL

GRATEFUL DEAD

BOB DYLAN
THE BAND
SUN RA
HOT TUNA

Rock music and trains, together? That might not seem like a likely pairing, but to members of the Grateful Dead, it seemed logical, especially for the group's folk-influenced music. In 1970, they traveled across Canada on a train as part of the Festival Express. This cover of *Relix* commemorates that tour.

Promoters lost money on the tour, but the musicians loved it. From coast to coast, they hung out, jammed, and drank. At several stops, they literally emptied entire liquor stores. By the time it was finished, the Festival Express was the longest-running party in the history of rock 'n' roll.

But despite the good times, members of the Dead had sorrows to face as well. As 1970 drew toward its close, they mourned the loss of loved ones. Jerry's mom died, and then Phil's dad. Then, on October 4, Janis Joplin died from a heroin overdose. All the Dead—but especially Pigpen—were devastated by the news. Nonetheless, the Dead released what may be its finest studio album, *American Beauty*, at that time.

The Curse of the Keyboard Player Begins

As they hit the road in '71, the Dead faced a problem: Pigpen was not well. A heavy drinker, Pig hit the bottle even worse after Janis died, and alcohol destroyed his liver. The band agreed Pig should take a break from touring; tragically, he never performed with them again. Pigpen died of liver damage. Losing one of their most vital members shocked the band. But Pigpen was only the first in what Deadheads call "the curse of the keyboard player."

The Grateful Dead needed a new keyboardist—and fast. Keith and Donna Godchaux introduced themselves after a concert in October. Keith dazzled Jerry with his playing, and Donna was a talented singer. They performed with the Dead from 1971 through 1979, years many Deadheads regard as the band's best decade.

Shakin' Down the Crowds

In July of 1973, the Grateful Dead played to the largest crowd ever gathered for a concert. More than 600,000 young people crowded into Watkins Glen Raceway for a single-day festival known as the Summer Jam. Some historians say Watkins Glen was the largest crowd gathered for a single event in the history of the United States: one out of 350 people living in America at the time attended the event.

It was the largest gig the Dead would ever perform—and for once, the group nailed it. The band played for five glorious hours, performing a number of favorites including "Uncle John's Band," "Casey Jones," and "Truckin." It was a golden day for the Dead.

The following year, the Dead introduced the wall-of-sound system. This awesome technological monstrosity was forty feet high and seventy feet wide. It held 600 speakers and 25,000 watts of solid-state McIntosh power, all piled together in one vast stack. The wall produced unbelievably clear, loud sounds—and equally unbelievable costs.

The Grateful Dead had a big sound, and it took big speakers to make sure everyone heard it at its best. For the Grateful Dead, that meant a 600-speaker, 25,000-watts wall of sound. With the big sound came a big road crew and a big expense. But the Grateful Dead didn't care as long as they got the best-possible sound.

Hard living began to take its toll on Jerry during the 1980s. His health worsened, and his band mates begged him to get treatment for his drug addiction, which he did. There were some good times for the group, though, such as a 1986 tour with rock icon Bob Dylan, seen here front row center.

The Dead already had an unusually large road crew; now it had to be doubled. Profits from each show went into a common pot that paid the road crew. For most of their career, members of the Grateful Dead saved barely enough to live on. What mattered to them was the sound, the artistic experience; making a profit wasn't so important.

The Dead Live at Pharaoh's Tomb

" **We now return our souls to the creator,
as we stand on the edge of eternal darkness.
In the land of the night
the ship of the sun
is drawn by the Grateful Dead.** "

So says the Egyptian Book of the Dead, a sacred text as ancient as the Bible. No wonder Egypt beckoned the Grateful Dead.

In 1978 the band's manager, Richard Loren, suggested an Egypt tour. The group was thrilled. Only one thing stood between the Grateful Dead and the Land of the Pharaohs: Bill Graham would have to finance the gig. The band members walked in on Bill carrying signs, "Egypt or Bust!"

The Dead members were enthralled by Egypt, especially after a private tour into the heart of the Great Pyramid, where they chanted together. They also enjoyed jamming with Egyptian musicians.

Finally the magical night arrived: the Grateful Dead played a live concert in front of the Great Sphinx. It was a huge moment and so—of course—the band played poorly. The group blew another big one, at least as far as the record company was concerned. Phil and Jerry were untroubled; it didn't really matter what they sounded like from their perspective. They knew the trip had a cosmic purpose.

Trouble Ahead

As the seventies ended, the Dead was as artistically vital as ever, but trouble lay ahead. Drugs that had inspired the band when it began were now wreaking havoc in the lives of its members. Keith and Donna were falling apart—destroying things and playing poorly. They had to leave the band and were replaced by Brent Mydland. Months later, Keith died in a car accident. Ten years after that, replacement keyboardist Brent died from a drug overdose, giving rise to the rumor that Dead keyboardists are cursed!

At this point, Jerry was addicted to heroin. As Phil says, "The drug gradually took over his life." At one show in '79, police officers guarded the stage because someone sent an anonymous death threat to Jerry. Then during the show, an unknown thief stole his heroin. As soon as the concert finished, Jerry got on the PA system: "Who . . . stole my stash? I left my bag here and you guys stole all my drugs!" The rest of the band panicked, because the police were still there—right in front of the stage.

The mid-eighties were hard on Jerry. In 1985, the rest of the band confronted him regarding his drug use, and he agreed to go to rehabilitation. The following year, he went into a diabetic coma. Recovering from this near-fatal illness, Jerry had to learn to play all

In 1994, the Grateful Dead was inducted into the Rock and Roll Hall of Fame. Jerry didn't make it to the ceremonies, so his fellow band members posed in the press room with a life-size cut-out of their leader. Jerry demanded that everyone who ever played with the group be inducted into the hall.

over again, but amazingly, Jerry and the Dead were back on tour only five months later. Despite these serious problems, the Grateful Dead could still create some wonderful music, as proven by its 1987 top-10 hit, "Touch of Grey."

The Tour from Hell

In the nineties, the Grateful Dead was just like the out-of-control train in its song "Casey Jones": the driver was high and headed for a crash. Ironically, the group sold more than ever; in 1993, the Dead was the best-selling concert attraction in the United States, in 1994, the group was admitted to the Rock and Roll Hall of Fame, and in 1995, its greatest hits CD, *Skeletons from the Closet*, went **platinum**.

Nonetheless, the artistic spark was fading, as Jerry was back on drugs and too addicted to play well. The band members felt responsible for their huge road crew—so the show went on, painfully and reluctantly.

The Dead's final tour, in 1995, has been called the Tour from Hell. At one show, two fans died when equipment fell, then three were struck by lightning a few shows later, and then a week after that, more than a hundred were injured when the huge set for the show collapsed. The whole tour seemed cursed.

One to Take Me Home

On July 9, 1995, the Grateful Dead played at Soldier Field in Chicago, Illinois. The performance was lackluster, but on one song, "So Many Roads," Jerry seemed to wake up. In a mournful, crystal-clear voice, he poured his aching soul into the words, "So many roads I know, *all I want is one to take me home.*" It was the last public appearance of the Grateful Dead. Jerry died exactly a month later.

Jerry Garcia had to deal with many life difficulties on the road to stardom. One of the biggest obstacles he had to overcome, at least when it came to playing the guitar, was the loss of his middle finger in a childhood accident. Despite the missing digit, Jerry's guitar playing was phenomenal.

Jerry Garcia, Broken Angel

Ker-chunk! Tiff brought the axe down hard, neatly whacking a log in two. Quickly, Jerry slid another log into position for his older brother to split. *Ker-chunk!* Another log halved. Jerry reached over with another piece of wood. *Ker-chunk!* "A-a-a-gh!" The two boys stared at Jerry's finger, barely attached to his hand, squirting blood beneath the axe head.

And that's how Jerry Garcia lost the middle finger on his right hand.

Destined from the Start

Jerome John Garcia was born August 1, 1942, in San Francisco. He was the son of Jose (Joe), a swing bandleader, and Ruth, a nurse. Jerry's parents named him after Jerome Kern, a composer who introduced a fresh, breezy style of melody to American music. With his father's blood and his famous namesake, Jerry seemed destined for a musical career.

Jerry was only four, helping his older brother Tiff chop wood for their family's fire-pit, when the accident happened. His parents rushed him to the hospital, and the doctor put a cast on his hand. Jerry waited impatiently to remove the cast and then, when the final bandage came off he shouted, "My finger's gone!" (His outstanding musical career is even more impressive considering Jerry's missing right middle finger.)

The next year brought a much worse tragedy to the Garcia family. Joe and Ruth were on a fishing vacation with Jerry in Six Rivers National Forest. Joe was fishing in the fast-flowing Trinity River as five-year-old Jerry watched nearby. Joe slipped on a wet rock and was swept underwater; it took fifteen minutes for other fishermen to pull him out. A doctor was nearby who attempted resuscitation but it was no use. At the age of forty-five, Joe Garcia died. Years later, Jerry admitted his father's death, "Emotionally crippled me for a long time. . . . The effect it had on me was really crushing."

To Learn and Love and Grow

In his adolescence, fortune shaped Jerry into the man who would influence the world with his music. His mother remarried and moved to Menlo Park. There, Jerry struggled through junior high, not because he lacked intelligence, but because he was bored with school.

Around the same time, two other important things happened in Jerry's life: he discovered pot and went to art school.

Since elementary school, Jerry had enjoyed drawing and painting. Throughout his life, he produced many fine paintings; if he had not chosen music as his major artistic outlet, he might have become famous for painting instead.

In 1958, he took lessons at California School of Fine Arts. The school was at the center of free-thinking San Francisco culture, so teachers there helped Jerry develop his outstanding gifts as a painter. At the same time, they introduced him to Beat philosophy and lifestyle.

In 1960, at the age of seventeen, Jerry joined the army. This wasn't the greatest idea for a guy who wanted to live like a beatnik, making art and music. His enlistment came out of desperation: Jerry was

Life as a young adult wasn't always easy for Jerry. He got kicked out of the army and was involved in an serious auto accident. Not long after the accident, however, he met those who would join him as the Grateful Dead. When Jerry and the rest of the Grateful Dead made music, he could put aside life's hardship.

bored with school and wanted to see the world. His service career lasted only briefly before the army kicked him out.

Entering adulthood, Jerry was drifting uncertainly through life when disaster struck again. At around one in the morning of February 20, 1961, Jerry was leaving a party in a car full of friends. Everyone, including the driver, had been drinking. The car was going ninety miles an hour when the young man at the wheel lost control and the car rolled over several times. Jerry's friend died in the crash. Later, Jerry said in an interview, "This was crushing. This was serious. . . . I was a changed person. It was cosmic."

Surviving the wreck pushed Jerry to move on with life, to do something significant. He pursued his music more seriously and soon met the people he would perform with the rest of his life.

Valentines of Flesh and Blood

Shortly after the car crash, Jerry met a smart, pretty fifteen-year-old girl named Barbara Meier. Like Jerry, she loved painting and the Beats. Jerry and Barbara dated, but Barbara's father forced them to break up.

Then in 1963, Jerry noticed Stanford student Sara Ruppenthal at a coffee shop—and it was love at first sight. Jerry called Sara a few days later and told her, "I need to be with you. I can't eat, I can't even play music. . . .You've gotta' come and be with me." She and Jerry were wed shortly after, and they had a daughter, Heather. Unfortunately, this hasty marriage was short-lived. Sara recalls, "We stopped being friends basically after we married."

Soon after, the Warlocks became part of the acid test scene, where Jerry met Mountain Girl (her birth name was Carolyn Adams). Mountain Girl and her daughter Sunshine moved in with Jerry at 710 Ashbury. As Rock Scully, road manager for the Dead, recalls, "They just fell in love. Jerry had that fortune . . . or misfortune, that when he falls, he falls hard." Hippie relationships could be confusing. Jerry and Mountain Girl lived together for the next nine years and had two daughters, Anabelle and Teresa. After another romance with a woman named Deborah Koons, Jerry and Mountain Girl were married in 1981.

Manasha Matheson started going to Grateful Dead shows as a little girl, and by 1987 had grown into an attractive young woman. She connected with Jerry during the band's 1987 tour, and in

December of that year they had a daughter, Keelin. By this time, Jerry had moved on from his earlier romances, but he promised he would be a better father to Keelin than he had to his other three daughters—but he didn't keep that promise.

In 1992, Barbara Meir re-entered Jerry's romantic radar; they felt the same chemistry they had as teens. Jerry didn't have the heart to tell Manasha and Keelin about this rekindled romance. He and Barbara flew off to Hawaii, leaving Manasha and his daughter without even a good-bye. They never saw him again.

Jerry was very popular with the ladies. Very popular! As much as he liked the ladies and they liked him, he just couldn't make a relationship work for very long. Sometimes it was his drug use that caused problems, and sometimes it was his roving eye that brought a relationship to a crashing end.

Jerry's second round of romance with Barbara Meir was intense but short-lived, because she confronted him about his drug addiction. Angered, he left her and reconciled with Deborah Koons. Jerry and Deborah were married at the time of his death.

The beatnik lifestyle was all about freedom—so beatniks impulsively loved and left significant others, and Jerry did likewise. Rock Scully said,

> **"Jerry Garcia was married to his guitar and . . . his human relationships suffered for it. None of the various women and children in his life could dispute that."**

The Singing Man Is at His Song

While Jerry Garcia is most famous for the Grateful Dead, that band was only one of his musical projects. Jerry was so talented, and so diverse, that one musical group—even an incredible band like the Dead—could not satisfy his creative cravings.

At the same time the Warlocks gathered, Jerry was one of the finest banjo players on the beatnik folk scene. He performed duets with folk guitarist David Nelson

In 1969, Jerry and David, along with several other musicians, formed a country band called New Riders of the Purple Sage (after a novel by Zane Grey). The New Riders were popular in the early seventies and produced one hit song, "Panama Red." They often played as opening act for the Grateful Dead. Along with Jerry, Phil and Mickey also played in New Riders of the Purple Sage, so for several years they performed double-time at concerts. Jerry left the New Riders in 1971.

From 1975 to 1995, Jerry played constantly in his "other" musical group, the Jerry Garcia Band. They performed a variety of musical styles ranging from psychedelic rock to jazz, folk, and blues. Like the Dead, the Jerry Garcia Band was **improvisational**—jamming, creating new versions of their songs at live events. Playing in one band is too much work for some musicians, but Jerry kept up with the Dead's incredible tour schedule and, for many years, performed with the Jerry Garcia Band between Dead concerts. He practically lived onstage.

Jerry had a lot of creative energy, and playing in one band—
no matter how good—wasn't enough of an outlet. In 1969,
he, Mickey, and Phil, as well as some other musicians,
formed New Riders of the Purple Sage, a country band.
Though the band was popular for a while, it only had
one hit record.

David Grisman, who played **mandolin**, was another of Jerry's
musician friends. Jerry nicknamed him "Dawg" when they played
folk music together in the sixties. Jerry and David produced the
albums *Pizza Tapes* and *Garcia/Grisman*, and played together in a
bluegrass band named Old and In the Way.

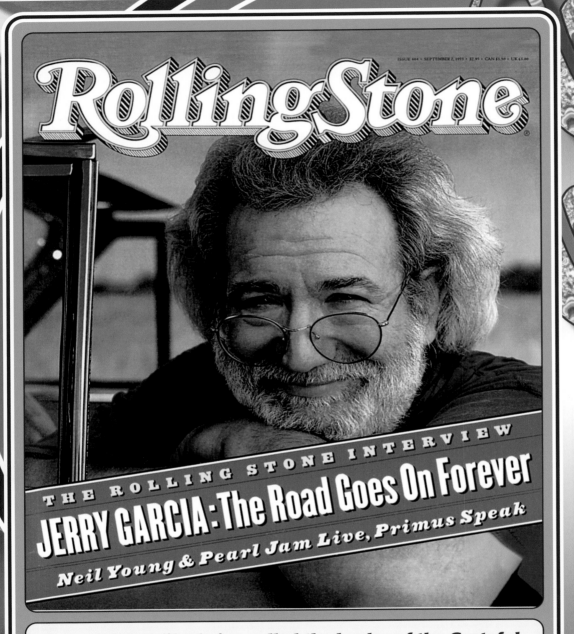

ISSUE 664 • SEPTEMBER 2, 1993 • $2.95 • CAN $3.50 • UK £3.00

RollingStone

THE ROLLING STONE INTERVIEW

JERRY GARCIA: The Road Goes On Forever

Neil Young & Pearl Jam Live, Primus Speak

If Jerry didn't like being called the leader of the Grateful Dead, it's for sure he wasn't comfortable being called a prophet. Deadheads regarded Jerry and the group almost worshipfully. And when Jerry appeared on the cover of *Rolling Stone*, the "Bible" of rock music, his image as prophet was secure.

Reluctant Prophet

The hippie movement died by the mid-seventies, with one enormous exception—Deadheads. Over the years, the crowds who followed the band grew larger. They gathered regularly, wearing tie-dyed shirts and headbands, smoking pot and keeping alive the carefree spirit of the Haight-Ashbury scene. So many people followed the group from city to city that Mickey Hart once said, "The Grateful Dead weren't in the music business, they were in the *transportation* business."

For the Deadheads who focused their lives on the concerts, the Grateful Dead was more than a band; it was practically a religion. Concerts were like church, with the band dispensing grace and Jerry Garcia serving as the prophet. According to a "Dead Head" quoted in Paul Grushkin's book, *Grateful Dead: The Official Book of the Dead Heads*:

> **"A Dead concert is my [sacred rite] and I eagerly await the festivities and rituals of cleansing. . . . The participation in each dance enables my spirit to transcend my body and mingle and rejoice with the spirits of all the other participants."**

Yet despite the fervor of fans like this who focused their worship on Jerry, he never thought of himself as a "holy man." He told an interviewer,

> **"These things are all illusions. Fame is an illusion. . . . Those things don't enter my life, I don't buy into any of that stuff. I can't imagine who would. Look at David Koresh [the leader of the Branch Davidians religious cult, many of whom died in a fiery conflict with members of the FBI in Waco, Texas]. If you start believing any of that kind of stuff about yourself, where does it leave you?"**

Listen to the Music Play

Late in the summer of 1995, Jerry entered Serenity Knolls, a drug rehabilitation center in California. There, while sleeping peacefully, he died of a heart attack on August 9, 1995. Dennis McNally said later,

In August 1995, Jerry Garcia died, leaving a void in the world of music. He hadn't lived a perfect life, but there could be no argument about his talent or the influence he had on music. President Bill Clinton called him a genius. Bob Dylan declared that Jerry "really had no equal."

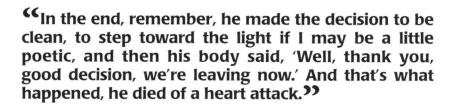

"In the end, remember, he made the decision to be clean, to step toward the light if I may be a little poetic, and then his body said, 'Well, thank you, good decision, we're leaving now.' And that's what happened, he died of a heart attack."

Since then, fans have exalted Jerry as an idol, and **detractors** have pointed fingers at him as an addict. Neither reality captures the true essence of Jerry Garcia's life: his music. As a human being, Jerry was neither better nor worse than most of us, but as a musician, he was a one-in-a-million talent.

After Jerry's death, President Bill Clinton commented to reporters that he and his daughter, Chelsea, represented two generations of Dead fans. He told MTV:

"He was a great talent; he was a genius. He also had a terrible problem that was a legacy of the life he lived and the demons he dealt with. And I would hope that all of us who loved his music would also reflect on the consequences of self-destructive behavior."

Legendary rock singer Bob Dylan said of Jerry:

"There's no way to measure his greatness as a person or as a player. I don't think eulogizing will do him justice. He was that great—much more than a superb musician with an uncanny ear and dexterity. . . . He really had no equal."

Jerry lived to play. If he wasn't performing with the Dead, he played onstage with other musical groups. If he wasn't onstage performing somewhere, he spent his days sitting with his guitar, creating new sounds. A philosopher once said, "Purity of heart is to will one thing," and the one thing Jerry focused on was music. As a newspaper reporter noted, Jerry was "our most improbable pop-culture idol, somebody to whom the playing matters more than the posing."

Jerry Garcia was a legend whose death affected many all over the world. His funeral was attended by musicians, family, and the Hells Angels. To many music fans, Jerry wasn't just the leader of the Grateful Dead, he *was* the Grateful Dead. His band mates decided the group couldn't go on without him.

5

The Music
Never Stopped

Jerry's death was enormous news. News bulletins flashed across television screens, and there were more than 10,000 postings on the Internet. In San Francisco, flags flew at half mast, and city hall displayed a tie-dyed flag. Mourning fans kept vigil at 710 Ashbury. His passing was front-page news on papers throughout the United States.

Other musicians and artists praised Jerry. David Crosby commented,

"Musicians and people who love music have lost one of the brightest, most articulate minds of this generation."

Ken Kesey waxed poetic:

"Jerry knocked a chink out of the wall and let the light shine through, and it's up to us to keep that light shining."

Bob Weir had a scheduled performance the night of Jerry's death with his own band, Ratdog. He told the audience,

"If our dear, departed friend proved anything to us, he proved that great music can make sad times better."

Sleep in the Stars

Jerry's funeral service took place at St. Stephen's church in Belvedere, California. Before the service, a line of Hells Angels drove up on their Harleys, went inside the chapel to pay their respects, then came out in black suits and helped with security. All the surviving members of the band, Jerry's three grown daughters, ex-wife Sara, Barbara Meier, Ken Kesey, and Bob Dylan attended the funeral, which was organized by his wife, Deborah. She did not invite Mountain Girl or Manasha Matheson.

Matthew Fox, an Episcopal priest, called Jerry

"a wounded healer . . . [who] is in a place where the ancestors gather, his musical ancestors, and one can only imagine the jamming going on there."

As the service ended, Reverend Fox asked the mourners to give Jerry one last standing ovation. They did so, weeping.

Jerry's body was cremated after the funeral service. On April 4, 1996, Deborah Garcia and Bob Weir sprinkled a portion of Jerry's ashes into India's sacred Ganges River. Weir wished his departed friend "May you have peace, Jerry, and travel to the stars." Eleven days later, Jerry's daughters and other close friends scattered the remaining ashes in the San Francisco Bay.

Jerry's tangled relationships led to an almost immediate legal battle. His estate, at the time he died, was worth nine million dollars. Within a few months, there were more than 38 million dollars in claims against Jerry's estate. More than ten years after his death, the fight over his estate continues. In January 2007, Deborah filed a lawsuit to gain access to unpublished tapes of Jerry's performances.

That Same Sweet Song Again

The Grateful Dead formally disbanded soon after Jerry's death, but that did not end the various members' musical careers.

In 1998, Bob Weir, Phil Lesh, Mickey Hart, and five other artists toured as the Other Ones. In 2002, a tour by the Other Ones was so successful that in February 2003, they named themselves the Dead (retiring "Grateful" out of respect for Jerry). The group toured through 2004, with Joan Osborne joining in vocals, and played several

Though the surviving members of the Grateful Dead knew that Jerry couldn't be replaced, they weren't ready to stop playing music together. Bob, Phil, and Mickey formed the Other Ones. In this photo, Bob (left) and Phil (right) are shown playing at the Further Festival in 1998. The Other Ones had a very successful tour in 2002.

shows together with Bob Dylan. Deadheads continued to come out in force, and magic was still in the air.

Bob Weir's band, Ratdog, continues to evolve, playing to sold-out shows and enthusiastic audiences. They play Grateful Dead tunes with the same improvisational flair and have added jazz elements to the songs.

Phil Lesh performs with his own group, Phil and Friends. In 1998, Phil had a liver transplant as a result of a life-threatening infection; thousands of Deadheads organized online to send him

The formal end of the Grateful Dead could not stop the devotion its most faithful fans felt for the group. The group's re-forming as first the Other Ones and then the Dead must have felt like an answer to a prayer to some Deadheads. Though the group isn't the same, Jerry's influence can still be felt in the music.

their prayers and well-wishes during the operation. Since then, whenever Phil performs, he encourages members of the audience to become organ donors.

Mickey Hart and Bill Kreutzmann also have a band, the Rhythm Devils, which likewise continues the Grateful Dead tradition of live performances. Mickey also works with the Smithsonian Institution to record the music of cultures around the world. He is a well-respected collector of percussion instruments.

Unending Devotion

The Grateful Dead story is both tragic and wonderful, sordid and miraculous. Dead biographer Dennis McNally said in an interview:

> **❝The Grateful Dead is this mysterious entity that is composed of . . . instruments and magic and music and all that good stuff. . . . [but] the Grateful Dead is something separate, and the only way to honor it is to tell the truth.❞**

It's not just fans who are showing their devotion and respect to the Grateful Dead. More than fifteen years after Jerry's death and the disbanding of the group, the Grammys came calling. The group received the prestigious Lifetime Achievement Award from the Grammy Foundation at the 49th Annual Grammy Awards ceremony.

Jerry and four other members of the Grateful Dead have passed away; and the remaining members who still perform cannot do so forever. Yet the band's musical magic may go on for decades, perhaps even centuries into the future. Unlike many other bands, the Grateful Dead encouraged private taping of its shows. For this reason, thousands of recordings of Grateful Dead concerts are available online and on commercial and privately recorded CDs.

As long as fans enjoy their music, the Grateful Dead lives on.

1965 The original band members form Warlocks; the name is later changed to the Grateful Dead.

1966 The Grateful Dead headlines at Bill Graham's Fillmore West.

The band releases its first single, "Don't Ease Me In."

The band, along with friends, move to 710 Ashbury.

1967 The group releases its first album, *The Grateful Dead*.

The group plays at the Monterey Pop Festival.

The band performs—badly—at Woodstock.

1969 A major concert is held in Altamont, California, and is disrupted by violence; the Dead decides not to perform.

Jerry and others form the New Riders of the Purple Sage.

1970 *American Beauty* is released.

1971 Keith and Donna join the band, Keith as keyboardist and Donna as vocalist.

1973 The Dead performs at Watkins Glen Summer Jam.

Pigpen dies from liver disease brought on by excessive drinking.

1974 The group debuts its Wall of Sound system.

1975 Jerry forms the Jerry Garcia Band.

1978 The Dead embark on the ambitious Egypt Tour.

1985 Band members confront Jerry about his drug use; he agrees to go to rehab.

1986 Jerry lapses into diabetic coma, but the group is back to touring just five months later.

1987 "Touch of Grey" hit the top-10.

The ice cream company Ben and Jerry's introduces the flavor Cherry Garcia.

1990 Brent dies of overdose.

1991 The Grateful Dead is the top grossing band in the United States.

1993 The Dead is again the highest grossing concert attraction in the United States.

1994 The Grateful Dead is inducted into the Rock and Roll Hall of Fame.

1995 *Skeletons from the Closet* is certified platinum.

The band performs in what will become known as the Tour from Hell.

Jerry Garcia dies, and the band is dissolved.

1998 Bob Weir, Phil Lesh, Mickey Hart, and others form the band the Other Ones.

2002 Two of Jerry's handmade guitars are auctioned for $850,000 and $700,000.

2003 After a successful 2002 tour, the Other Ones rename themselves the Dead.

2006 The Grateful Dead is awarded the Lifetime Achievement Award at the 49th Annual Grammy Awards.

Albums

1967 *The Grateful Dead*

1968 *Anthem of the Sun*

1969 *Aoxomoxoa, Live/Dead*

1970 *Workingman's Dead, American Beauty*

1971 *Grateful Dead* (also known as *Skull & Roses*)

1972 *Europe '72*

1973 *History of the Grateful Dead, Volume One, Wake of the Flood*

1974 *Grateful Dead from the Mars Hotel, Skeletons from the Closet: The Best of Grateful Dead*

1975 *Blues for Allah*

1976 *Steal Your Face*

1977 *Terrapin Station, What a Long Strange Trip It's Been*

1978 *Shakedown Street*

1980 *Go to Heaven*

1981 *Reckoning, Dead Set*

1987 *Dead Zone: The Grateful Dead CD Collection (1977–1987), In the Dark*

1989 *Built to Last*

1990 *Without a Net*

1991 *Infrared Roses, One from the Vault*

1992 *Two from the Vault*

1996 *The Arista Years*

1995 *Hundred Year Hall*

1996 *Dozin' at the Knick*

1997 *Fallout from the Phil Zone, Live at the Fillmore East, Selections from the Arista Years*

1999 *So Many Roads (1965–1995)*

2000 *Ladies and Gentlemen . . . The Grateful Dead, View from the Vault, Volume One*

2001 *The Golden Road (1965–1973), Nightfall of Diamonds, View from the Vault, Volume Two*

2002 *Go to Nassau, Postcards from the Hanging, Steppin' Out with the Grateful Dead: England '72, View from the Vault, Volume Three*

2003 *Birth of the Dead*

2003 *The Closing of Winterland, The Very Best of the Grateful Dead*

2004   *Beyond Description (1973–1989), Rockin' the Rhein with the Grateful Dead*

2005   *The Complete Fillmore West 1969, Fillmore West 1969, Rare Cuts and Oddities, 1996, Truckin' Up to Buffalo*

2007   *Live at the Cow Palace*

Number-One Single

1987   "Touch of Grey"

Videos

1981   *The Grateful Dead Movie, Dead Ahead*

1987   *So Far, Making of Touch of Grey*

1992   *Backstage Pass, Infrared Sightings*

1996   *The Concerts, Ticket to New Years (Oakland Coliseum, New Year's Eve 1987)*

1997   *Downhill from Here (Alpine Valley Music Theater, East Troy, July 17, 1989), Grateful Dead Collection*

1998   *Anthem to Beauty*

2000   *Live in Concert, View from the Vault (Three Rivers Stadium, Pittsburgh, PA, July 8, 1990)*

2001   *View from the Vault II (RFK Stadium, Washington, D.C., June 14, 1991)*

2002   *View from the Vault III (Shoreline Amphitheatre, June 16, 1990)*

2003   *View from the Vault IV (Oakland July 24, 1987 and Anaheim July 26, 1987), The Closing of Winterland*

2004   *The Grateful Dead Movie* (remastered and extended DVD)

2005   *Truckin' Up to Buffalo, Dead Ahead* (expanded DVD)

Awards

1994   Inducted into the Rock and Roll Hall of Fame.

2006   Grammy Awards: Grammy Lifetime Achievement Award.

Books

Dalton, David, and Rock Scully. *Living with the Dead*: *Twenty Years on the Bus with Garcia and The Grateful Dead*. Boston, Mass.: Little, Brown and Company, 1996.

Jackson, Blair. *Garcia: An American Life*. New York: Viking, 1999.

Lesh, Phil. *Searching for the Sound: My Life with The Grateful Dead*. New York: Back Bay Books, 2005.

McNally, Dennis. *A Long Strange Trip: The Inside History of the Grateful Dead*. New York: Broadway Books, 2002.

Parish, Steve, with Joe Layden. *Home Before Daylight: My Life on the Road with the Grateful Dead*. New York: St. Martin's Press, 2003.

Troy, Sandy. *Captain Trips: A Biography of Jerry Garcia*. New York: Thunder's Mouth Press, 1994.

Web Sites

arts.ucsc.edu/Gdead/AGDL
Annotated Grateful Dead Lyrics by David Dodd

www.dead.net
The Official Site of The Grateful Dead

www.gdhour.com
The Grateful Dead Hour

www.myspace.com/philandfriendsofficial
Phil Lesh and Friends on MySpace

www.phillesh.net
Phil Lesh and Friends

www.rat-dog.com
The Official Ratdog Home Page

www.rexfoundation.org/rex_home.html
Rex Foundation Home Page

www.rhythmdevils.net
Rhythm Devils News

www.rukind.com
Grateful Dead Music Forum

beatific—Having to do with a state of utmost bliss where the individual directly experiences divine reality.

bespectacled—Wore glasses.

bluegrass—A style of country music from the southern United States and usually played on fiddle, banjo, guitar, and mandolin, and featuring close harmony.

blues—A style of music based on African American folk music of the early twentieth century.

detractors—Those who speak ill of someone or something.

dyslexic—Having dyslexia, a learning disorder characterized by difficulty in understanding written language.

enthralled—Delighted or fascinated.

eulogizing—Praising someone highly, usually after death.

improvisational—Having to do with performances that take place in an unrehearsed, spontaneous manner.

improvise—Make something up on the spot.

mandolin—A stringed musical instrument of the lute family, with a pear-shaped body and with four or more pairs of strings.

platinum—A designation that a single has sold one million copies, or that an album or CD has sold two million copies.

Kenneth McIntosh is a freelance writer living in northern Arizona with his wife and a small menagerie of pets. He last saw the Dead, along with Joan Osborne and Bob Dylan, in 2003 at Darien Lakes, and enjoyed the Ratdog show in Anaheim in 2006.

Picture Credits

page

2: Icon Image Express
8: Custom Medical Stock Photo
11: UPI Photo Archive
12: Photo Trend Int'l
14: New Millennium Images
17: UPI Photo Archive
18: Arista Records/Icon Image Express
18: Star Photo Archive
20: Arista Records/Icon Image Express
20: Photo Trend Int'l
23: Rare Pics Library
24: Foto Feature Collection
26: Foto Feature Collection
29: Rare Pics Library

31: New Millennium Images
33: Photo Trend Int'l
34: Arista Records/Icon Image Express
36: Starstock/Photoshot
38: Popperfoto Archive
41: Arista Records/Icon Image Express
43: Rex Features
45: UPI Photo Archive
47: New Millennium Images
48: UPI Photo Archive
50: Arista Records/Icon Image Express
53: KRT/PressLink
54: Arista Records/Icon Image Express

Front cover: Warner Bros. Records/Star Photos